Jenn,

Enjoy!

— [signature]

Coming Out of the Chaos
by SJ Whenham

© 2021 SJ Whenham

All rights reserved. No part of this publication may be reproduced, distributed, or transmitted in any form or by any means, including photocopying, recording, or other electronic or mechanical methods, without the prior written permission of the author, except in the case of brief quotations embodied in critical reviews and certain other noncommercial uses permitted by copyright law.

ISBN: 978-1-7359389-1-2

Produced by Kindship Group
Printed in China with Soy-Based Ink on Acid Free Paper
sjwhenham.com

For my Mom and sister, who have lived through,
and come out of the chaos with me.

Between these pages lies
        the culmination of moving through
        turbulence of young adulthood.
The marks of all the moments of chaos,
the people that created them
And the woman I've become because of them.

PART I	1
PART II	49
PART III	73

Part I

I think of my father
And I think of wheel wells peppered with red rust on an old Dodge.
I think of my father
And the salt and pepper of his handlebar mustache. In desperate need of a trim
I think of my father
And days wrapped in his strong arms.
The ones that protected me from dragons and the bad guys

I think of my mother
And the quiet certainty of a house that was always ready between visitors
I think of my mother
And the honesty of making banana bread
A moment of rare solace before the oven dings.

I think of my parents.
And the backbone of our lives
After every crash, every shattering, every white light followed by chaos

A new life is borne.

Soldered and welded back together
Here we are, today
Here and now
A life rebuilt and not fallen upon.

This is us
The quiet contemplation of our being.

Spring is here and everything slowly comes back to life.
Hello beautiful, wake up lovely.
Leaves on trees sprout and open with timid grandeur
Every living thing must allow itself time to open under the pressure of life
springing forth around it.
Trees are jungle gyms once more.
When plants awaken from their frosty slumber
So do we.

Spellbound
magic.
Magic.
In the stars,
in the rising sun,
in the mountains this place it needs
quiet, time and healing.
It is creating and coffee and the dark red of wine and love
the mist settles on the peaks of mountains begging to be touched by the clouds.

Grandma's kitchen cabinets
Where china never sat in a backlit awkward hutch pushed up against one wall.
The set of mugs did not remain a set for long.
Always fresh flowers on the table.
Clipped, sheared and arranged so that the season out the kitchen window was viewable from the hall.
Sunflowers, peonies, roses and daisies.
Fragrant florals mixed with cinnamon and nutmeg.
A seat with one rip in the cushion.
The inevitable fight over it ensued.
Cuts cleaned,
dirty hands and
faces washed and
dinner served on the worn in china.
Because every meal,
           every moment,
           here was special.
And so, every day was a good enough day to use the china.

Don't go toward the light they say,
but the light feels like the safest place to be

THE JOURNEY

My mom came over to my apartment one spring afternoon with the sole purpose of finding my great grandma's house, which (we hoped) still stood in the city of Edmonton.

I had been living in Edmonton now for five years. The harsh winters and shock of the summers had grown on me. I remembered the day that I moved so vividly. I drove up the highway, only a few hours, and thought that I'd relocate for a year, maybe two at most, and be back in Calgary. But the universe had a different plan in store in for me.

In those five years, my mom has only come up here a couple of times. Once, when I was living with a boyfriend who had succeeded in hiding his mental illness and ensuing medications from me. We stayed in our apartment that left its mark above a jazz bar and Chinese food restaurant.

More recently, my mom came to Edmonton looking for something other than me. She came looking for her grandparents, my great grandparents. Tryntje (Tina) and David Fokema.

Tina - or Tiny as we affectionately called her - was my great grandma. She was from Holland, her first language was Dutch. She spoke with a very harsh, thick accent until she passed. Her story is one that is rife with change, and a desire to move forward, giving the best to her children.

TINA

The boat was hotter than you would expect. I had hoped for more of a breeze on deck, and at least some ventilation leading down to the areas below deck. My two children were screaming already. Kees, only 6 and Ann, just 4. My youngest child, yet to join this world, was restlessly moving around. This one could sense my nervousness. David was just behind us, ushering us into the small quarters that would be ours for two weeks. Two weeks. The passage between the Netherlands and Canada.

Shifting on the restless tides between a place I had always known, I had only known, and a place of questions.

Our quarters below deck consisted of two single bunk beds for us, and another set that had already had a Spanish family of three occupying its space. Olive skinned and black haired, they offered an intense opposition to our family.

Despite the obvious differences, the same nervousness was palpable throughout our families. Mostly downcast, but often darting eyes told the stories of where we had come from. Across the swaying ocean, and in hearing the gentle slaps of the waves just outside our windows, every breath between us told a story.

I was in my second trimester of my third pregnancy. Weary, I struggled to get comfortable in those days on the boat. The small bunks did little to ease my aches. The uncertainty of knowing what was on the other side of our journey did little to quell the building nervousness in my heart.

At the beginning of World War II, I was happy to see that the Netherlands had declared neutrality. That declaration did not stop Nazi Germany from launching an attack on the Netherlands and Belgium. This overran most of the country quickly. I had heard David's concern about the lack of preparation on the part of the Dutch army, which turned out to be true. It felt like a dream, the fighting. We were so far from the chaos and danger. People in Rotterdam saw the first fighting, but up in Oosterbierum, we went about our days.

I turned our house into a home, sweeping and baking. Hanging small pictures on the walls and mending the tattered curtains. David tended the fields that brought his hands home to me calloused and bruised. Our kitchen table was the center of my life. Bread waiting to be baked rested there and the good wine was shared when company came to visit. I healed scrapes, and mended the cut on David's right eye when he took a ball to the face playing with Kees. Laughing, and intensely proud of his son for the great throw, he hardly noticed how deep it was. The scar remained, a reminder of a moment that truly mattered.

I hurried my children to Church and the market, as though the rest of my people were not in turmoil. I bandaged scrapes and cuts, smoothed down dresses, and braided Ann's and my hair into smooth plaits as though we were not in the middle of a world war.

Life does go on, in the midst of chaos. In the midst of loss, grief and days that will define us, small things still need to be done.

And now we were on a ship. Transforming our lives, going into the unknown, moving forward into a new life. But my babies still needed their bedtimes stories. They still needed kisses for their knees and encouragement when playing.

Life does not stop amid change.

Life does not stop amid chaos.

I did not know how different Canada would be. I was willing to follow my husband wherever if it meant that there would be no threat of war or extremism. I believed in a better life, one that would catapult my family into peace and prosperity.

TODAY

Nearly 70 years later, my mom visited Edmonton, looking for something more than just me.

We drove around the northern part of the city looking for Grandma Tina and Grandpa David's small house.

There it was. Still standing, a mighty force of quiet amid the last standing trees and a newly paved highway.

I had a single small memory of that house. I was of course, too young to really know the history that was kept between those walls.

My memory of that house was playing Ker Plunk with Great Grandpa David on the dark brown shag carpet in the front room. The large windows overlooked the driveway into the farm. The house sat on an acre and my great grandpa loved every inch of that land. Ever the dutchman, not a single piece of that land went to waste. He tilled, and toiled, grew a huge garden of peppers, tomatoes, lettuce and potatoes. Huge raspberry and strawberry bushes flanked the back of the house. What he grew out of the ground, my great grandmother turned into elaborate feasts in the kitchen. We had homemade bread, berry crumbles with homemade vanilla ice cream. Loving the land was the original investment in their lives.

What if memory lane was a real place?
If memory lane was a real place I don't know that I'd ever come home.
To feel your soft hands,
skin as delicate as a butterfly's wing,
a small taste of heaven emanates from this moment.
If memory lane was a real place
I wouldn't have to feel badly about not spending more time with you.
I'd have the opportunity to do it again and again.
Spending hours strolling, laughing and learning.
If memory lane was a real place,
I don't know that I'd ever come home.
And then what?
And then I'd never know who's memory lane I'm on right now.
Who would come here?
Seek me out as their chance at a do-over.
I wouldn't know,
I'd be too busy living in the past.

If I do not allow the shadows to engulf my small frame
and follow the slouching line of my shoulders,
my downcast gaze.
It has no power
I straighten myself up
and shout to the heavens that
sadness has no place here
reach for the hearts
reach for the love
reach for the contemplations
and for fuck's sake believe them and do not rest until you know this for certain.

She could feel the breeze as it tickled her skin
heightened her awareness of her sunburnt forehead
the sound of the rustling stalks of wheat
soothed her they offered transcendence
oh beauty oh nature oh sun oh moon oh stars
she stares in silence
in wonder
in love
as the landscapes unravelling before her very eyes
the smell of childhood
of long walks home she was transported into another time
another place in the distance where the past no longer held onto her present
it no longer had hold of her future
her mistakes washed away as sure as the rains bring forth new life
in the farmer's harvest season
and moon line haystacks stood unmoving.
unflinching the painting before her had had power over her being

as a child
I was afraid of what most are, the things that go bump in the night.

But now, I am most afraid of their truth.
These children are not afraid to be exactly un-apologetically truthful.
They do not hesitate to tell me I look like shit and they get away with it because they do not understand tactfulness.

This is the most frightening.

                        These children have taught me what I'm afraid of, and what I'm not.

CRUMBLING

I remember the day that my parents announced their divorce. I use the word 'announce' because that is what it felt like to me, a grand proclaiming of what the future was to hold. The future that they had envisioned, but my sister and I were just in that moment coming to understand.

The couches in our living room were pushed together, we had built a fort the night previously. A vast expanse of cushions and pillows encased by the backs of chesterfields held us tight as the news was delivered to us.

Cindy? Should we drop the bomb? My dad's disembodied voice carried from the kitchen

Lacey and I both knew what the bomb was.

It had been coming for months, maybe closer to a year. Time feels suspended when you are a child.

You're getting divorced? My shaky voice, one that I did not recognize came through in the couch cushion fort of the night before, the night when things were the same and safe.

No, no. just separated. It's not the same thing. It's temporary. I promise. We just need to try something new. Try something out.

I could tell in the body language that my mother held that it wasn't temporary. Strong and proud, defiant to our tears and a ripple of wavering and questioning that held just beneath the surface of her resolve.

From the moment that the announcement was made, a shuddering went through the house. A wide chasm opened up in my universe as I clung to my little sister for any semblance of normalcy.

Dad moved out. A truck pulled up to the front of the house, and a futon from the basement bedroom was thrown haphazardly on in the bed of truck, forming a kind of u shape that resembled a hot dog bun. I remember that I thought it would be funny if Dad had jumped into the futon and called out:

Don't worry! It's a joke, I'm a hot dog, but I'm your dad and I still live here.

Instead, he got into the truck with his hot dog bun futon mattress and meagre belongings and drove away.

We lived in a small town. A town where everyone knew everyone. The corner store, where my sister and I would walk to in the summer for five cent candies (the Stop 'n' Go), was just a short shuffle down a red shale pathway outside the elementary school.

A single traffic light marked the entrance, and the most desired exit for myself and all my classmates. It was the place you came home to, but also the place whose permanent exit was on a countdown, a timer until the graduating class finally walked the stage.

When my mom and dad 'separated' the kids on our street were sympathetic, if not somehow, understanding. Even though they knew nothing of this kind of thing. My sister and I were surrounded by families who made it work. Who stayed with each other for the kids. Who overlooked, and turned a blind eye to the quiet calculation and dissatisfaction of their lives.

My mom is a lioness.

Even after things with my dad disintegrated, a sense of family and togetherness permeated our home. The phone hanging on the wall by the kitchen counter rang as her friends were calling her, checking in. I can't forget that my mom was only 32 - the same age that I am now, with two children, in the midst of a 'separation' from her husband, somehow holding it all together.

Mom got jobs, coached our soccer teams, and went back to college while raising two daughters. She was completely present. All the time. When I needed help with my homework (I was never good at math or science), she was there. A quiet force, not always knowing what she was talking about when it came to 6th grade long division, but always willing to figure it out with me. When I was unsure of how to decorate my room (that was my sanctuary), she measured my decisions with a trained eye. She suggested my movement of a chair six inches to the left and my Polly Pocket collection to be stored away in my closet to prevent clutter. Reclaimed items from other areas in our home became ottomans, stools and night tables.

When mom couldn't purchase, she made. Birthday cakes, Halloween costumes, candies, clothing. Even things for the house: curtains and duvets, tablecloths and couch covers. She knows her way around a sewing machine.

She made the wedding dress and a whole ensemble of bridesmaids dresses for a woman in our town. I say woman, but the reality is she was probably much younger then than I am now. And I stop to wonder, how would that have made my mom feel? So young herself, with young daughters, sewing the dresses that a woman only 10 years my senior would be getting married in? Because she had daughters, did she feel like my sister and I were on borrowed time? Before we were walked down the aisle to our husbands?

Where I grew up, this is what you did. You graduated high school, and married your high school sweetheart, or anyone that came by and told you that you were pretty. As if taking Biology 20 somehow prepared you for the quiet disappointment of a marriage bed. As if mass was an appropriate precursor to an understanding of the bond between two people. As if English 30 gave you enough of a repertoire to understand life. The writings of Proust and the stanzas of Lord Byron, the prose of John Irving and the lessons of Harper Lee did nothing to prepare me for what I was going to lose in the fire, a short 10 years from the crumbling.

Mom went back to school after her and dad split up to study Criminal Justice. She had never gone to college prior to this, but it seemed like a small price to pay to do something just for herself, the first time in her life that she had put herself first. She wanted to become a cop. And she would end up teaching DARE classes at my school. Mom put herself out there in college, becoming friends with her professors and running a study group from our kitchen table. One of the regular study group attendees, a young guy with wispy brown hair named Gary would bring packages of the biggest Costco muffins. I always got a chocolate one to share with Lacey. Gary ate the poppy seed muffins every single time. At the end of their certificate, and so many poppy seed muffins later, Gary failed his very first drug test at a job he had applied for.

Mom threw us the best birthday parties. She spent days baking cakes and getting excited to celebrate my sister and I. Lacey has an early summer birthday, mine is in the fall. As much as possible we would make sure to line up the party with a day of good weather so that we could have a water balloon fight. Balloons are cheap to buy and provide kids with endless hours of entertainment. There would be hot dogs on the BBQ and the cakes shaped into whatever we wanted. For my birthdays, the mass of the cake was a dome shape, with a Barbie stuck right through the top. The cake would be meticulously decorated to resemble the Barbie's huge princess dress. I wanted nothing more in life than to have a huge dress made fully of cake. Something I could walk around in and reach down when I needed a quick snack.

CHASM

My dad lived in a small house across town after the "separation." What is now a short walk, felt like the largest chasm that was un-walkable as a child. Peeling white paint adorned the outside of the house, accompanied by a sad looking, drooping basketball hoop nailed to the detached garage. Through the gate, on the back of the house, was our entrance. An overgrown backyard, rife with dandelions in need of a wish stood, reaching for the sun. A lean-to shanty stood in the far left corner of the yard. Begging to become a clubhouse. In the late 90s, a clubhouse was the dream of every child. My clubhouse consisted of inflatable furniture and an area for creativity, flanked with purples and pinks of every texture, my clubhouse appealed to all the senses.

The inside of my dads house at this time consisted of a lot of empty rooms. A sad futon in the living room, where we would watch The Simpsons, with my dad muttering quietly:

Your mom wouldn't want you to be watching this.

We watched it anyway.

A small bistro set inherited from someone was all that sat in the kitchen where we hastily consumed our microwave meals. A place that use to symbolize gathering, a place that brought conversation and deep theological discussions over coffee and cake became a place that we hurried to be rid of. Eat quickly so we can go back and watch TV. Something to numb the reality of all that was happening. Where my mom would create and keep her hands busy to keep us unfocused, my dad did the opposite. We were left to our own devices. He took care of us, made sure were fed and had what we needed. But he was depressed. Only putting in his time until he could no longer take his mind off the reality that he had created and we were gone.

My dad did the best he could at the time. And his best would only get better and better as the years wore on.

My dad has always lived with a sense of chaos in his life. His upbringing was not one of storybooks and fairy tales. Dropping out of school and leaving home at a young age to work and seek solace on the road will do wonders to encourage wariness. Bathed in chaos and clothed in a sense of uncertainty, he trudged forward seeking a life that would settle him down.

After the 'separation' our house grew somber. It was quiet. I threw myself into books. Anything I could find to create an escape from reality. I travelled back and forth from the town library. Pedalling on my bike hoping that maybe, just maybe, if I went fast enough, some new continuum would open up beneath me, swallowing me whole into it.

My childhood was not bad. My parents loved me, and still do. But every child wants the same thing, to be lost and then found again. Doting parents that begin a search party for their children. Even though their children are just downstairs, safe and sound. Safe and sound doesn't always feel safe and sound to a child.

As a child I longed for adventure. That longing would take me in my adulthood across seas and continents into the great divide. While in this small town, I discovered adventure in the smallest of corners, in the quietest of spaces. Between pages and rolling down the sides of what I considered to be huge mountains. But I see them now and they are what they've always been, rolling hills that you'd barely break a sweat walking over.

COMPANIONS

My sister and I could not be more different. Not just at the core of who we are, but in the way that we see and react to the world. Lacey is a fighter. She sees the world in black and white. Where I've always seen a varied palette of greys.

When I retreated, Lacey threw herself into an extrovert's world. Sports, friends in big groups, and getting dirty on our Grandpa's farm was the antidote to her reality.

Where I retreated into the stacks of books at the library and into a world of fiction, Lacey was chomping at the bit to create her own life, one that was firmly rooted in the present and real world.

I clung to the things that we shared hoping that it would create a sense of certainty and belonging, even if only just between the two of us.

That didn't really work out the way I hoped. Not because we were too different, but because I was trying to be something I wasn't. In the hopes of being enough for someone else. When all I really needed to do, and all I really needed to be was myself. And I was more than enough for Lacey, just as I was.

Lacey saw me as the older, wiser one. Though she didn't show it. Her love is represented through teasing and poking fun at others. It's always been that way. She would not let up and protested: IT'S A JOKE whenever I (or anyone) got too offended.

In the beginning it never seems this way, but as an adult, I expect her review of this story to be:

You're crazy, I love it.

Nothing like a lifetime of backhanded compliments to really grow a thick skin.

Broke the curse with your own two hands
                                            cracked
opened wide for the air to graze against.
                                      a plate shattered on a kitchen floor.
Porcelain in pieces crying out when blood is drawn from a missed piece
 remaining on the floor
The curse remains.
                                  next time, I'll get it.
Next time.

The room reeks of an underwater grave.
The dust floating slowly to the earth.
A beam of light.
Singular.
Unwavering.
Not here for long but I am enveloped in this opulent darkness.

In the whispery quiet of my living room.
Next to the flickering lamp illuminating
my dusty "soon to be read" stacks of books.
I am reminded of the unstoppable.
Unwavering passage of time.
Of my own life.

Sentiment

a moment.
Fleeting sentiment that cloaks the darkness
why does the rule of life have to interfere with the need for love?
A waterfall of emotion rushing over my face
my body
drenching me in the reality that is now the presence of

what is here
what is tangible
I pick a leaf off the ground and grind it between my fingers trying to understand its importance.
Even after it turns to dust that floats away and coats the pavement in its remnants
floating away in the wind.

A smell of stickiness in the air
the quiet flutter
I won't soon forget
do not forget to allow yourself the gift of space,
place and tangible quiet.

time painted with the brushstrokes of passion.
Time passed through the waves of sound and desire.
Colors that move invisibly through brain waves.
Evoking the strange passions and emotions that make the intangible rooted in reality.
The movements of the soul through a night sky when released from earthly torment.
The colours of a sunset.
The smells of fresh cut grass and ocean surf, so lightly kissing the shore no matter how many times it is sent away.
The dancing brushstrokes painting through time,
on a lazy Sunday,
a busy weekday afternoon or a coldness of heart.
I can play. I can sing. I can listen,
but sometimes, I cannot understand.
Not even when it is my own voice.
My own song, my own words.
Someone please tell me what I mean.

Mirrored
another side,
another story,
another leap of faith,
another chance at glory

Open Love

Heart. Greens and blues.

The sways and swells of the ocean they are deceptively green and even more deceptively blue.

Black obsidian and onyx

those that close and burden are not welcome here

and do not guide toward the

love that springs open the heart and throat chakras.

My world on my back
items neatly rolled, folded, and tucked into
a 55 liter red backpack
A gift from a friend,
became the only constant on planes,
carousels in international and regional airports
the desert
a rainforest.
Ol' Red came with me.
carrying my world on my back
until she got too heavy
always to be found right where I left her.

A quiet breeze,
wings flapping,
clouds shifting,
reveals the sparkles
blue blacks, purples and pinks
a sky fraught with terror
Opens up above and
highlights its own power.
The shifting coloured nimbus above
reflected in the depths of hearts.

The hum inside a seashell –
a movement of quiet it
shifts silence that is changeable
the cold of the shell pressed
and held and anticipated
against the flush of the face
it is the sound of everything that world could be
Sigh.
Move.
Sigh.

Sparking treetops
a small door to the entrance of things left unsaid.
Feelings, words, thoughts,
felt but never said.
A bottle of emotion,
cork pushed down tight.
A glitteringly insipid morning
frosted with dew and a shimmer of magic
    - fairy tale quality

a warmth that moves like an orb.
> -Luminous

Bouncing swaying
           ominous, eerie here it comes
                        - heat

The open, romanticised ocean
salty flecks connect with my skin

beneath me
life teems and here I am again alone on this voyage with no compass
just my heart and soul for guidance
                alone out here is the best way to be
no one else's time clock or concerns, out here I am free.

skin against skin.
My soul reaches for yours.
Please don't leave me here.
Don't leave without me.
This is the first
this is the only time
I know that your flesh
and body keeps true to mine
women not alone, finally.
Women as one.

Part II

Lessons that we learn in the dark
his breath smells sweet.
The lingering of beer that has been drunk over many days.
Decisions that have not been mine made over & over.
The stick that brings children is on my legs.
I want him gone.
Take your stickiness and your sweet breath with you.
There is no emotion between us.
Only the regret of drinking and the wish that I would have stayed home.
After dark all is quiet.
Warm beer only tides me over until the fix I know there is one more in the bedside
table.
I reach over in the dark, my fingers fumble.
Knowing not what they touch.
But I know the pill right when I find it.
Into my mouth. And into oblivion. I slip.
The darkness stays into the morning.
I wake up to him already inside me.

Our second date.
On the first, we held hands. Laughed.
And tonight, somehow, you had drifted from calling me a treasure,
you now sit in silence.
Endless swiping,
back and forth,
left and right,
you can sometimes miss the one that stares across the table at you.
Becoming familiar with your transparent act.
Better now than later I suppose.

Cleanse me with blood.
Every shift of the moon and star patterns -
here you are cleansing the body
and soul
stripping away the faded times of tears shed
and disappointment written on my skin
 the moon rises,
and then,
so do I.

The cover of night - movement between the shadows.
I am aware of noises, rustling, what could be a predator.
Hold your keys between your knuckles
I saw that on Oprah once.
carry a whistle
yell fire, not rape,
my mother taught me.
- Fearfully female.

My breasts like targets identify me.
I am a woman walking alone
a target
a victim
prey.
Not without a fight
– Fearfully Female.

Sex Dreams

the thing I love most about being a woman is the lack of evidence of sex dreams
                        they are all mine
in the morning they keep me company in the
                        honey light and
after my third cup of coffee at 3 pm
                        the gentle caresses and
way my body undulates at the thought

I get to choose who I let into those moments

I don't get to choose who I have them with.

I was awkward
the day it happened
I was not aware of its magnitude
nor did I have the ability to deal with it for many years.
I would not have the wherewithal to understand its rippling impacts
it was both beautiful and terrifying
the monsters lurked below the black stills
there was a lochness, an Ogopogo inside of me
after surfacing, there was no hope to thrust it back below the surface.
creating swells on the shore

I remember approaching the moment like the lake in May
it will still be cold
      with trepidation
       testing with toes
I was ready for the moment
      not the aftermath

in a state of melancholy it began
    waiting
      waiting
        waiting
for what I assumed would be the main event
it didn't come
beating of fluid water on the solid walls of rock
                eroding away any fears
when they should have been growing
when the water broke it created a dam that would not stop
      I knew
      I knew
           I would never be the same.

Smoothly,
slowly,
the pull of honey and
years to move out of the past.
Your voice is calligraphy.

Desperate.
Despite your need for me, my skin cries out for you.
My shoulders arch toward the sky that is your mouth.
Take me, taste me and roll me on your tongue.
     - fuck

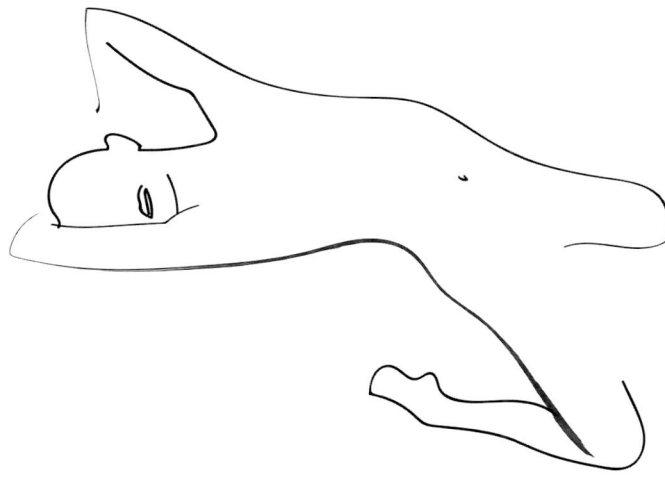

The ties that connect but do not bind
Who were you to me?
So long ago, in a place that I wouldn't even recognize now?
Who were you?
In the field of dreams, where long stalks of wheat rustle in gentle wind?
Where the roughness of the brick walls follow around the dirt paths and the blanketed forest floor?

Connection in a place that heightens the astral plane of time and love and being.
Invisible strings glitter in imagination that run all over the world and connect those who feel most lost.

Connection between the forest and the marketplace.
The car show and the library, slowly, quietly, bringing us together until we crash into one another.
A being in a place we know nothing of, but we know we are somehow, home, and here to stay, for a moment at least.

Leaving as quickly as we came, our worlds too different
too vast
laid across the expanse of who we've grown to be
And who we've worked so hard to become

The military meets the boardroom in a dance of unsustainable chaos.

I ache for longevity but know that that will never be the case.
so an understanding settles across my weary bones and I become aware of the reality.

That chaos and heartbreak, and the deep swelling up and down of inhospitable love makes me insatiable.
Makes me realize that this is not me, nor is it who I want to be.

I will wake up with you one morning, many years from now and not recognize myself.

You will extinguish my fire, my passions, without even knowing it.

I feel it happening now.

So let the ties that connect us run their course

And let them go

No matter the cost today, for the hopefulness of tomorrow.

brace for impact.
The impact against the reality of my heart.
A rush of falling stars in my belly.
Tumbling and turning and shaking and skipping.

Time is short.
It always is.
The impact is worse when it begs acknowledgment.
The anticipation is worse than the event itself.
This we know as the hard and naked truth.
Boom went my heart,
boom went my soul,
and boom went my voice (when she allowed it).

Echoing so loudly over the precipice of the cliff upon which I stood
getting to the ground
holding onto the edge and all the while
shouting out my love for him
the hard earth digs into the palms of her soft hands and fingertips.
Scraped skin.
Broken nails.
How do the injuries worsen when hanging on?
Yes - sometimes even more so.
let go and hope

- hope that someone is there to catch you when you fall
          if not pick up the pieces of yourself and be a
stronger wiser woman for it
               howl as you fall but
                    especially as you climb.

NAH

I was sitting on the floor in the apartment that belonged to the youth pastor and his wife.

I was 21 and struggling.

Struggling with what it meant to be a woman, what it meant to be Christian, what it meant to love and have a relationship with God.

My mom had remarried, we had moved to a big city, and I was still struggling to find the community that I had in our small town and so longed for in our new home.

I did not miss the small town in Southern Alberta that we left, in fact, I was glad to get out of there. There had been many instances of bullying (more on that later) and general toxicity in my friend group (again, more on that later). But now here I was, a ship adrift in this huge city (a million people seemed huge) and no where to anchor to.

So I sought out a community in churches. I could never quite find what I was looking for.

I once asked someone, a devout Christian, how do you know that we are on the right track here? How do you know what believe is the right thing?

Her answer: oh I just know. I just know that there is one true God. And we are right for worshiping Him.

Well, just knowing isn't a good argument, no matter how much you believe it. You have to have some more concrete reason don't you?

I guess not.

But that's what I needed. I needed someone to debate, someone to argue, and someone to have more of a background in theology than just this random woman who happened to have married a pastor and is blindly following him into the abyss.

I didn't like that. In fact, it made me move further away from the church. That was the second last step away for me.

The last was this moment:

Talking about sex in a bible study.

The pastor's wife had come into her own pious self and was asking all of us about our sexual history. It was unusually quiet. People who are born again generally don't want to bring up the past. Generally, we are trying to wipe that slate clean. Generally, we don't want to talk about it. But one woman's dedication to judging can be stronger than the need of the collective.

A small blond woman speaks up finally, she had made it very well known that she had been a virgin until marriage. It was what defined her whole god damn personality. The pure one. So chaste. Big whoop.

With a shaky voice, she admitted to having touched herself in the bath. She felt so dirty because she was enjoying her own body without her husband present.

I had lost my virginity at 19, three years before this moment. I could feel myself spiraling: if this married, pure, chaste as fuck woman was a dirty whore for flicking the bean in the fucking bathtub then there is no hope for me. I'm a ruined woman. A jezebel. A whore.

But suddenly the absurdity of it all came into focus. The need to control the female form under the guise of Christianity seemed so ridiculous in this moment.

I lost my virginity in the back of Alex's parents car and guess what? Jesus still loved me.

This woman was so upset at having not honored the sanctity of marriage, but I saw her behaviour as a liberated act of self awareness and love.

Within the confines of Christianity, I'm being told that I can't have sex before marriage, that sex is a sacred act between two people. People who have been joined together in the eyes of God and before the church.

But I'm also being told that sex is a really important part of marriage, and according to Cosmopolitan sex acts are the "10 ways to keep your man interested."

So now I'm confused. I have to save myself, I have to preserve my purity, but I also have to know what I'm doing, and what I like, and how to please my husband. So where am I supposed to get that experience without experimentation?

I nah'd right out the there. There had to be more people here who understood the flawed nature of figuring out your shit. Surely, I wasn't this horrible person just because I'd succumbed to the flawed nature of being human. Feeling chastised for fumbling through life and committing to the mess was not for me. These were obviously not my people.

I learned a valuable lesson that day though. The power of my voice. The sinking feeling of not using it. I left that day and never looked back, but I did not use my voice in that moment. It was the breaking point of my silence. This sparked a journey to find my voice and shout it from the rooftops. Some of that which you are now reading between these pages.

Swirling snow laps at my soles
I seek refuge from the winter winds in the chapel's expanse
glittering items all carefully laid out on tables crowing the naves.

A choir loft filled up with things for sale
Item no one needs but are required to ring in the season
the colours seem more dull

Disillusionment broken open on a piano bench

A hot cup of coffee on Christmas morning always has to be spiked.
Kahlua.
Baileys.
Whiskey.
Anything to get through the fact that Santa isn't real.

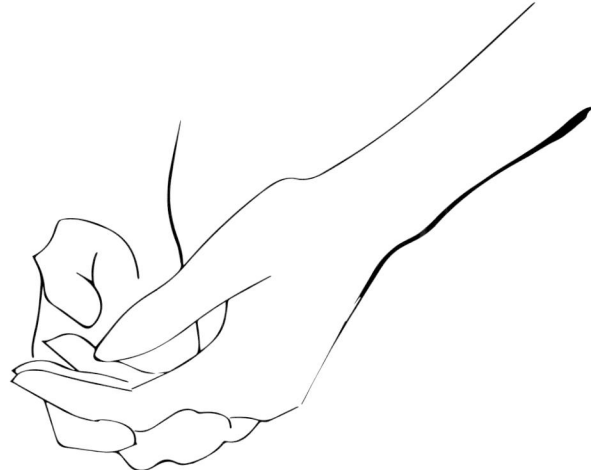

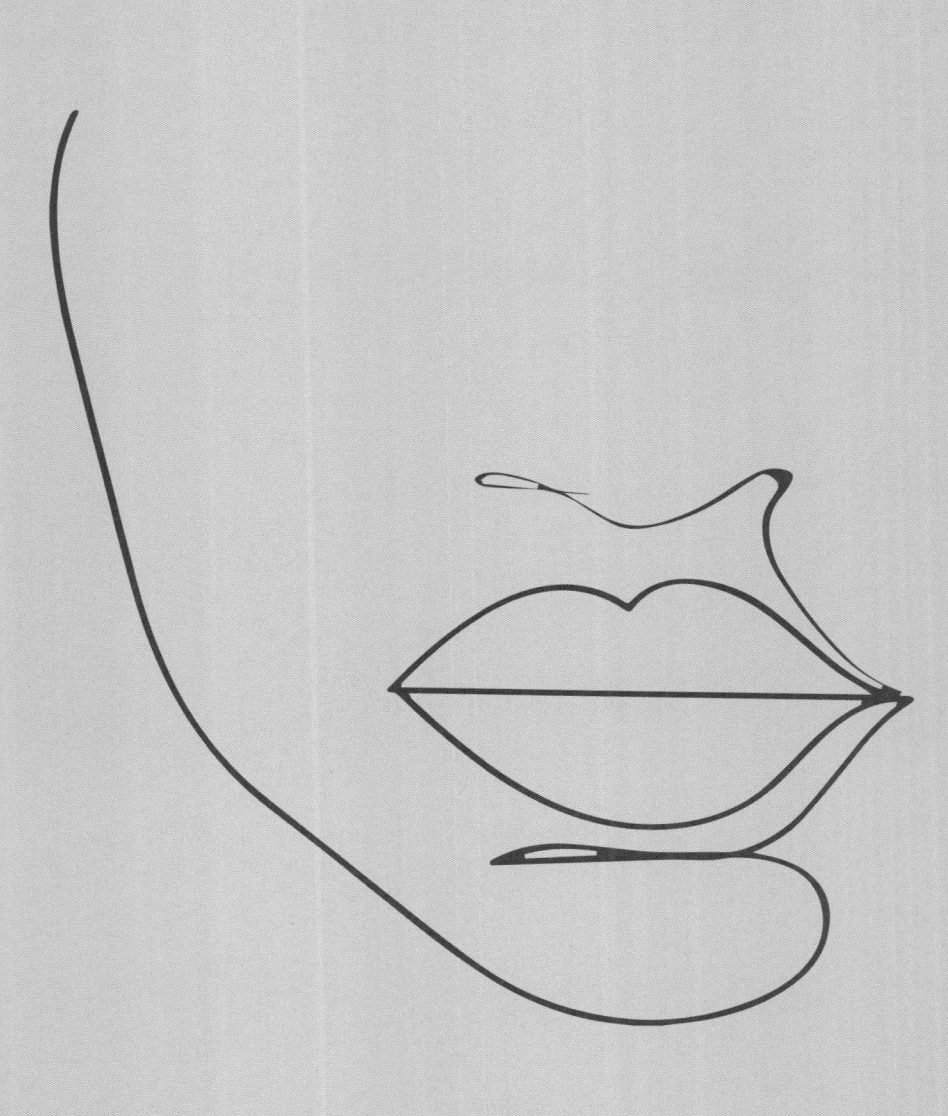

Part III

10 000 Emerald pools

glittering greens blues that ignite the throat
gasping for air.

>   Knowing the words that must be spoken
>   Deep clear waters
>   Deep murky soul

Endless, bottomless, boundless.
Finding yourself on the way to the bottom is always possible.

Both the mark of class and a whore
    - pearl necklace.

A poem on indulgence
I wait for you, moving slowly through the silence
your absence adheres to the walls
I wait for your touch
one that engulfs
envelopes
surrounds me fully
I work through my quiet loneliness knowing
you will never come even though I wait.
Every day the sun comes up and every night goes down again and
I indulge just by standing and waiting for you.

A tall brick house
               a treasure trove.
I sit in different rooms,
spaces,
surrounded by life,
glinting beauty,
textures,
and find myself lost in a world of pirates,
princess & stone walled taverns

                                      - Anxious to linger.

Bodily Harm –
tenderness and softness but not in the way that you consider weakness.
Tenderness, bodily harm.
What do you know of as strength?
The woman that has been through it.
She has seen it she knows

the pain the struggle the reality.
She is not tender.
She is not soft.
Just her flesh is.

The air is heavy with quiet.
An engulfing,
surrounding,
all encompassing weight of words left unsaid.
Silence decorated with sadness

Meadow sounds

earth mother
she is our sustainment
our divine goddess
pouring forth life,
but we still claw to survive.

The bruise on her body was convincing of an accident
she would have to replace the expensive lampshade.
Purple and discoloured and reminiscent of her reality
it hangs onto her body too long
and onto her heart longer

We just met.
But something is different.
I say that every time.
And then I realize. You are more of the same.
                - I've been here before

Ache -

the slow rolling of thunder -
cloud cover over a soul/ inner spirit.
Threatening the small ray of light
which is then squashed by the light drizzle drenching your
skin

        hair standing on end.
Goosebumps.

Cold that seeps through your physical being
and into a place where it cannot come out.

A wise, bewitched woman once said: out damned spot.
And I finally know what she means.
Out damned doubt
out damned fool
out damned cold of heart.

Out damned woman who believes she is not enough.
Allow yourself to feel the ache begin to ease.

The texture of hope
drips from my skin and
deep
deep
cleansing breath
a breeze caressing my face.
Hope is here dripping from my skin.

Dominion at your feet

                    I lay my needs down.
          Looking only for how to live in harmony
   crying out for a space in which to feel love fully on the floor
I don't think I'll find my answers here shrouded in darkness and
            cloaked in sentiment of what was once.

Vaulted - your back arches before my waning glance.
Giving under the weight of my heart.
You reach slowly into the ground breaking,
my heart is unknowing to emotion
that brings me back down to earth.

the wind has beaten and twisted your spine
centuries old movement

      leaving you looking like glass from a far.
I put my hand on you

          running it down over a curve and get a sliver
      I was naive to think that just because you'd been shaped differently
you've lost all your power.

Increased energy
soft humming,
where two worlds collide,
across the planes of time,
vibrations that increase,
hold, hold, hold,
increase and
hold, hold, hold.

Where the universe's lifeblood springs forth,
and a tiny movement,
a shift in orbital mass,
and direction changes.

This is the place where clarity looms just outside our door.

The place where a knowing, where a being comes to life.

This is the place that I needed to be, where I need you to be.

This is the place that increases understanding.

Increases knowing, increases being and increases our energy.

Sore muscles.
The ones that make me woman.
They cramp and cry out.
I am just an unwilling participant in this rite.
only now just understanding this power lurching in my womb

Carrying my heart in this cavity
the weight of it rocks me back and forth
wave beating against the hull of a ship
Shielding from the exhaustion of love and brokenness.

The countdown

I had been waiting for him for over 30 minutes it was our first date I owed him nothing. I should leave.

10. A shop door closed
9. The neon sign turned off
8. I took a deep breath
7. Someone turned the corner
6. He was walking toward me
5. There are roses in his hands
4. He is coming closer
3. These are for your
2. Sorry I'm late
1. All is forgiven I am a pushover.
Or I am in love?
Who knows the difference really?

in the obsidian night, I cry out to the moon in rage.

    - torn apart.

Inklings
    - that shifty shadow it lurks behind a curtain.
That quiet doubt
the silence of what you already know.
To be true
    - but will you listen?

oh what is it to be sightless.
Robbed of what you think is yours by right
your entitlement leaves you blind
and leaves you begging not to see
but to be seen.
To be understood but not to understand.
To be happy
whatever you think that it is happiness means.
I would be so lucky to be sightless, but not blind.

All the ways we tried to change.
It's a dangerous game.
that game of change
the game of pushing ourselves to be someone
we haven't gotten to know yet
all in the name of not waking up alone
it's a dangerous game.
learning to hide and speak censored.
The risk is waking up next to someone and not knowing yourself

23:55
so close to the next day.
That's what time it is.
It is sometimes never, but almost always so fucking close to the next day
like that somehow creates a clean slate
but it never really does it's just the next day of whatever has taken place before
what has become more real in the evening light.
The continuance of a buzz - an oncoming headache.
That's what 5 minutes to midnight really feels like

Sunlight
beating and unyielding
she shines giving life and killing

Those who cannot withstand her power
Burn

And here we are on sun kissed sidewalks.
Pavement drenched in regret
   - keep going

who was I?
all those years ago, when thinking twice did not yet exist
and my womanhood gleamed against an onyx coloured sky.

I was the moon,
bright,
a lantern glowing on the side of a
brick soot covered building,
offering safety and solitude,
even through it never truly came to that.
        - dark with memory

How to tip the scales:
be bold and brave and full of courage
tip the scales through your never-ending
honesty and one day you'll find yourself in a forest
speaking to the wildlife and they will listen to you

Mist and decay
soft wisps of shadows
float over hard surfaces
but death and heartbreak
linger just below.

Sync - breathe in you wish your howl will become mine.
Don't move.
The moon is here.

Why do you deny yourself heaven?
that horrible recurring feeling.
That nagging self doubt and question:

>am I enough?
>Am I good enough for this thing?

The question we never ask is:

>am I the best version of myself?

That should be the more important question.
But instead I ask, comparatively,
am I enough?
Am I the best in the group?
How do I measure?
Stack up?
Look standing next to these people that I consider better than me?

They are all - more mature, together, smarter.
I deny myself heaven because I won't stop comparing.
I won't stop analysing.
Heaven becomes a distant dream.
         Heaven.
                  Heaven.
                           Heaven.
Heaven is closer than I think though.

Heaven is here.
It is without self doubt,
without trepidation.
Without fear.
Heaven is right here at home.
Curled up under blankets.
Heaven is within myself, within grasp.

                       The biggest favour
                       I could do for myself
                       Is stop denying heaven

Facts are bigger in the dark
all truth is told more genuinely after the lights turn out.
There is no need for shyness no one can see your face.
Only hear your voice.
Be careful not to give yourself away in a slight tremble.
There is less of a reason to be frightened in the dark.
It is one thing to say a thing, but quite another to reveal a thing.
The dark protects against that.
How frightening to tell the truth with the light on.
Under a beating sun.
when your soul is exposed and can be snatched out of the air
pulled away from your being and crushed
between the mocking fingertips of another.
The clandestine way we meet in the dark
where a human touch is a human touch
breath is breath
truth is truth and absolute.
No lie can be told here, and no half truths can be forgiven.

We live.
Concerning others
are they fed
clothed
tired
well,
but no one asks if we are.

Mother, sister daughter:
are you well?
Do you have enough?
to eat
to breathe
to love?
Do you feel free?

                 - Female fastidiousness

The words I swallowed
are not nearly as painful as the ones I wish I had swallowed
swallow only words that are said with the intention of malice
save swallowed words for your writing
know when and with whom to spit
words swallowed will rot away in your gut.

Colonial tree lined streets dripping with the heavy scent of magnolias.
I wash the grit of the city off my skin at the end of the day.
A sinister, unsettling political climate,
marked by people who can't afford a doctor's visit,
and wait at death's door.
The grim reaper roams these streets in broad daylight preying on the innocent and weak.
The impoverished.
And I sit here, writing and reading in a café.
A rolling buzz and the heat of the sun on my skin.

Onto Bliss

time to focus.
Time to praise
time to give thanks for bliss.
That's going to be the word of the day,
for the rest of my days.
Blissful,
bliss out,
bliss in my soul.
Awoooo
I am going to carry bliss with me everywhere
that means ditching the phone,
hydrating,
having an afternoon bath,
or an afternoon beer and
finding authentic comfort in my skin.
Too much to ask for in one day?
Nope.
Not here, not today.
Miss me with that un bliss full attitude.
Focus on self love.
Coming home to my body and
my soul and
my spirit.

I tried to be softer
understanding is a virtue I could never attain
everyone who doesn't think like I do is wrong
sensitivity is not to be tolerated
                                    but I am trying.
Trying to be softer
move into shades of blue
more clouds
                                    shifting in a light breeze on a warm summer's day.

My heart, is sore

    -Longing

This place, weakens my soul
spirit crying out to howl.

    -I leave

Back to the woods and the crunch of leaves
where freedom to practice engulfs me

Forget you -

forget you, the woman who through she could not
forget you the woman who believed she was not enough.
Forget you
and forget your believed shortcomings
the ones that you hung on the wall and took such good care of all those years.

You are a goddess.
Forget everything else you know
or everything else you think you know about yourself.

And remember that the world should be so lucky to hear you roar.
so forget your old self
The one with self doubt

Anger
resentment
negativity

Today is the time of moving on and believing in the self that is whole.

So forget you.
Forget that girl and her worries.

>One day, you won't even recognize her,
>I promise. Today is the day to introduce yourself
>to the reflection you see in the mirror.

You are strong
you are capable.
You are confident
and as vast as the Butchart gardens in July.
You don't need me or anyone else to tell you that, because you know.
So forget you
you are now free to rebirth yourself

Move on to the relationships that push you forward and don't slow you down.
If you aren't being lifted, you are being suppressed.
So forget you, forget the people that don't hold you up.
But most of all, forget your old self, the one filled with self doubt.
Forget that.

Make Room

make room for love

room for kindness

for understanding and compassion

make room for quiet for the days that stretch into nights

and the nights that stretch into mornings

make room for alone time

make room for meditation

make room for yourself

Water power is greater than horse power
water smashing against the rocks and
I cant help but think:
what would that do to my soft body?

A poem on forgiveness -

let it go.
So that relief can wash over you like the large blast of a sudden tsunami engulfing the shores of everything in its path. Replaced with the cleansing waters of forgiveness.
Smooth like glass and languid like honey
the quiet calm of moving on.
Breathe in and out and let the tides fall at your back.

She must first build it.
The altar.
The altar that must be erected for herself.
Before she can bow down to herself as woman
herself as prowess
as lioness
as queen
she is goddess
but first she must build
before she bows
she must and she will
Build it.

For once, there are no words.
For a writer, this is important.

ACKNOWLEDGEMENTS

This book would not have been possible without the unending support of my best friend, Kyla.

To everyone who encouraged, proofread, edited, provided feedback and lifted me up through this process, thank you.
I am blessed that there are too many to name.

To my publishing consultants, Kindship Group: you gave me creative freedom and direction when necessary to bring this to life.

ABOUT THE AUTHOR

Coming Out of the Chaos is SJ Whenham's first published work. She has been writing for 15 years and is passionate about both poetry and prose.

She lives in Stony Plain, Alberta with her fiancé, cat and dog.

Photo courtesy of: Phoebe Marinakis